IRISH MUSIC FOR FLATPICKING GUITAR
MADE EASY
BY PHILIP JOHN BERTHOUD

MW00442528

Audio Contents

1	Factory Girl	16	The Butterfly
2	Paddy's Green Shamrock Shore	17	The Rocky Road to Dublin
3	Planxty Irwin	18	The Rakes of Westmeath
4	Carolan's Dream	19	The Irish Washerwoman
5	The Parting of Friends	20	Caliope House
6	The Derry Air	21	The Cliffs of Moher
7	The Star of the County Down	22	Sergeant Early's Jig
8	Whiskey in the Jar	23	The Jolly Beggarman
9	Oh! The Britches Full of Stitches	24	The Rights of Man
10	John Ryan's	25	The Wren Hornpipe
11	Kerry Polka	26	The Boys of Malin
12	The Rakes of Mallow	27	Miss McLeod's Reel
13	The Road to Lisdoonvarna	28	The Merry Blacksmith
14	Tatter the Road	29	The Star of Munster
15	The Runaway Jig		

Online Audio   www.melbay.com/21398BCDEB

1 2 3 4 5 6 7 8 9 0

Visit us on the Web at www.melbay.com — E-mail us at email@melbay.com

Table of Contents

Introduction

This book and recording contains a selection of 29 traditional Irish tunes. They are arranged for easy flat-picking guitar, roughly in order of difficulty. The music is clear and easy to read, but for those that don't read music, the music is written in guitar tablature as well as standard notation. Some readers may be unfamiliar with **first time endings** and **second time endings**. Look at Paddy's Green Shamrock Shore on page 5 and notice the brackets containing the figures 1 and 2 halfway along the third line of music. Imagine you are playing the tune and you come to the first bracket with the number 1 in it – this is the first time ending. Play the two bars under this bracket and you'll reach the repeat barline (double line with two dots), which tells you to repeat this section (from the third bar of line 2). Now you're playing this music for the second time, which means that you'll *skip* the first time ending when you come to it and jump straight to the second time ending (the bracket with the 2 in it). First time endings are also known as first time bar or first time bars – likewise for second time endings. Most of the tunes rise no higher than the fifth fret. Each tune is featured on the accompanying recording, played through at a slow tempo 2 or 3 times.

When working on a particular tune, spend time listening to the recording, in order to familiarize yourself with the sound of the tune. With traditional music, a great deal is picked up by ear. Have the tune going round in your head before attempting to play it. This will make the process more natural and rewarding.

On the recording, each new tune will be "tapped-in" so that you know when the music will start. Aim to play along with the recording as soon as you know a tune well. They are all recorded quite slowly so as to make play-ing along more manageable.

With traditional Irish music it is quite normal to play a particular tune through more than once. In some of the tunes in this book you will find a final note/notes printed in brackets – these notes are designed to be left out when playing a tune for the last time. They are only played if you are going to go back to the beginning of a tune and repeat it. Likewise, some tunes are shown with a single note at the end that is clearly marked to be played the last time through.

Below is an effective plan of action for tackling each new tune:

1. Listen to the tune on the recording a couple of times.

2. Listen to the tune again, this time following the corresponding music in the book.

3. Look more carefully at the music and make sure you understand what you need to do to play it.

4. Now, working at your own pace, begin to play the tune. How slow or fast you go is not important. What is important is that you take care to play the right notes.

5. Check back to the recording to hear what it should sound like.

6. Keep practicing the tune, getting to know it better.

7. When you are at the stage that you can play the tune from beginning to end, you could try playing along with the recording. If you don't get to the end, don't worry. Set yourself targets such as reaching the end of the first line, then the sec-ond line of music.

8. When you know it well, see how much you can play by memory. Some players do this more naturally than others.

Thanks to Dave Wade for mixing and mastering the recording.

Factory Girl

Paddy's Green Shamrock Shore

Planxty Irwin

Carolan's Dream

The Parting of Friends

The Derry Air

The Star of the County Down

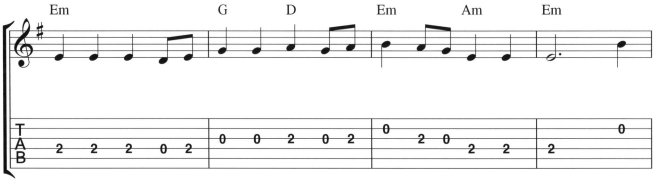

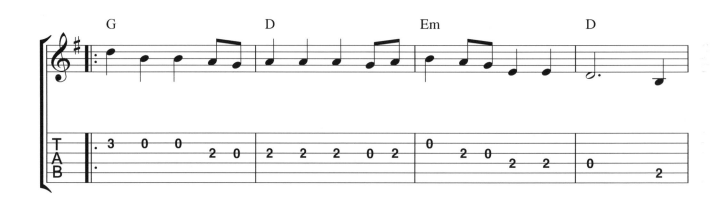

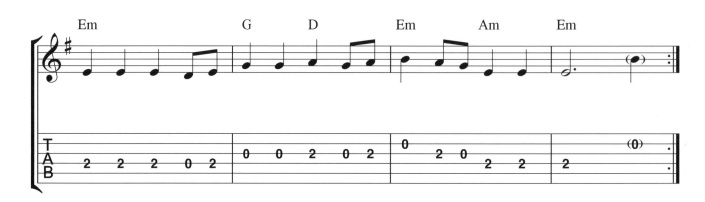

Whiskey in the Jar

The Britches Full of Stitches

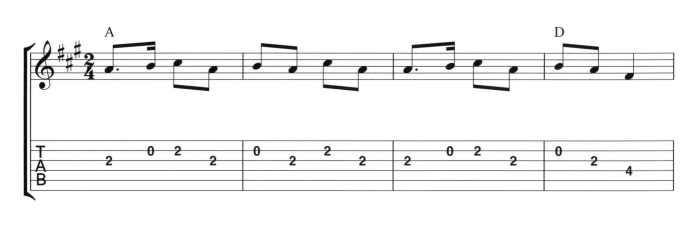

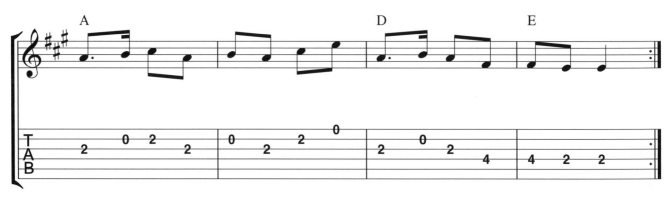

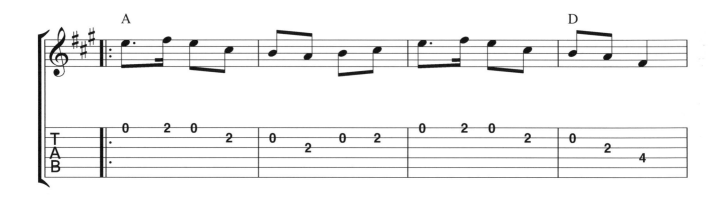

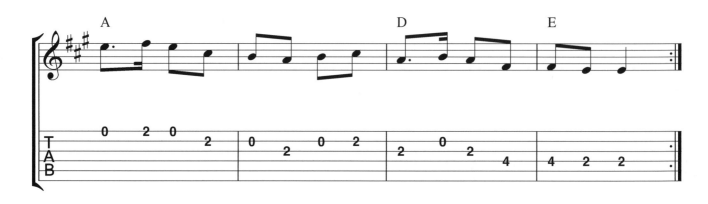

John Ryan's Polka

Kerry Polka

The Rakes of Mallow

15

The Road to Lisdoonvarna

Tatter the Road

The Runaway Jig

The Butterfly

The Rocky Road to Dublin

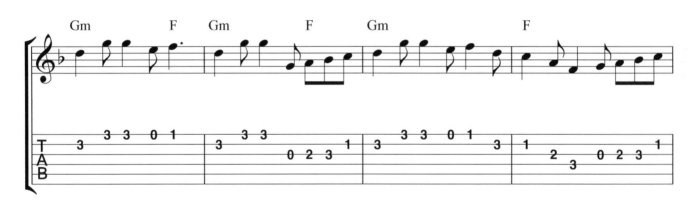

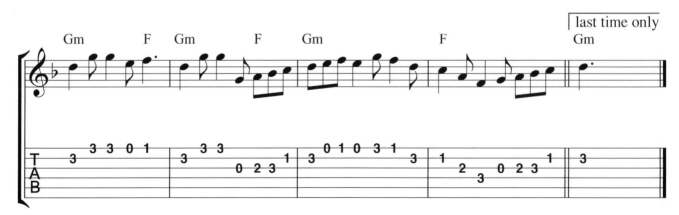

The Rakes of Westmeath

The Irish Washerwoman

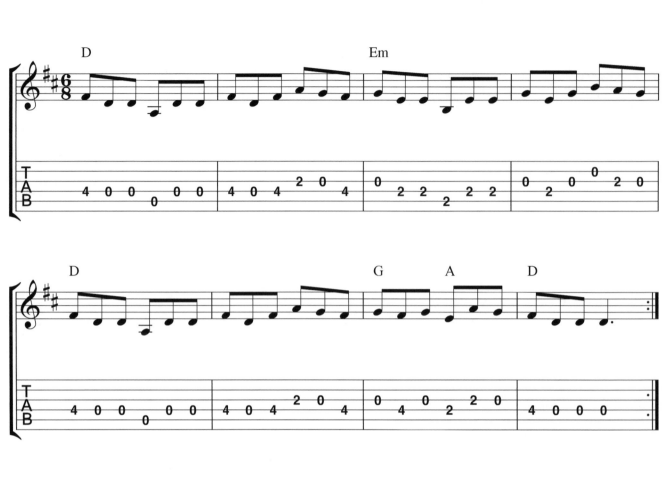

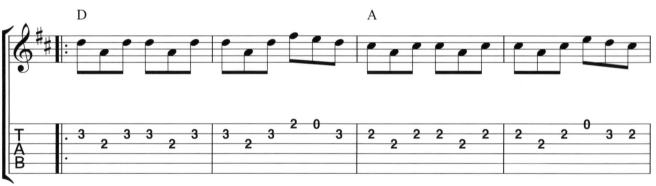

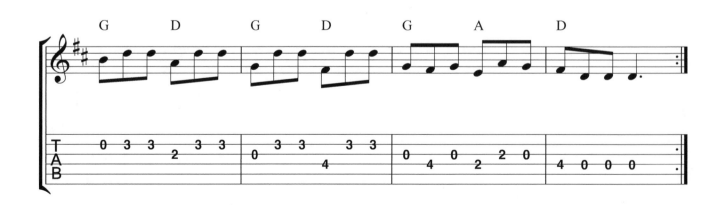

Caliope House

The Cliffs of Moher

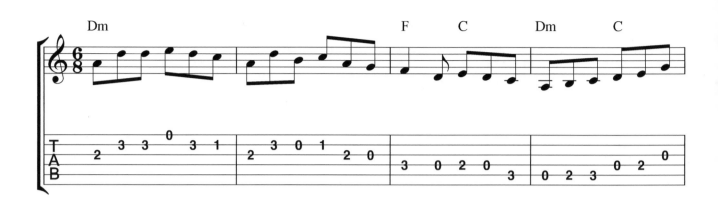

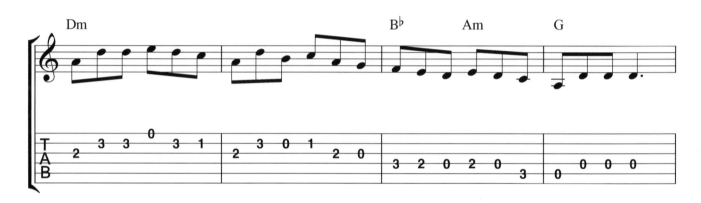

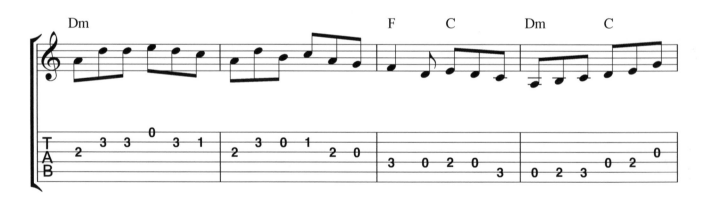

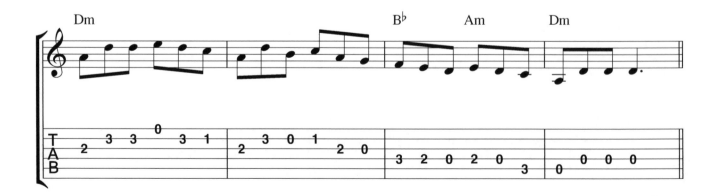

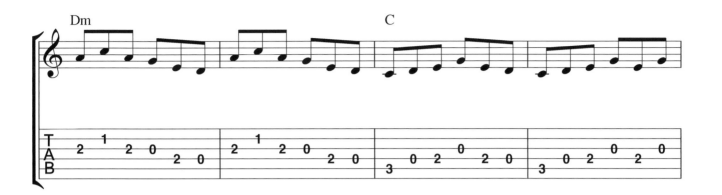

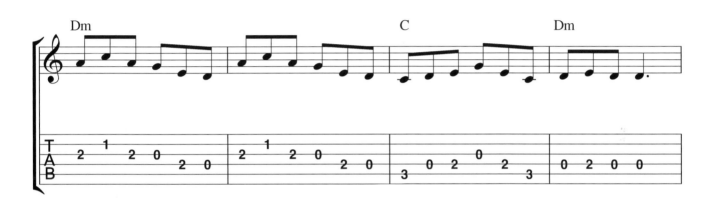

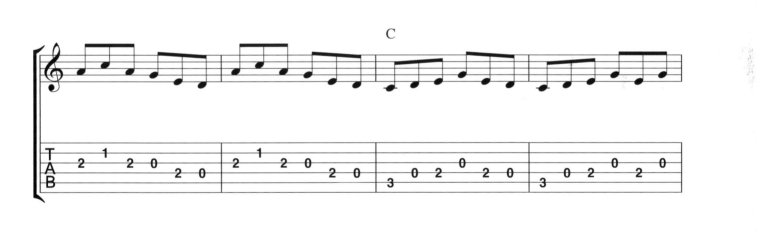

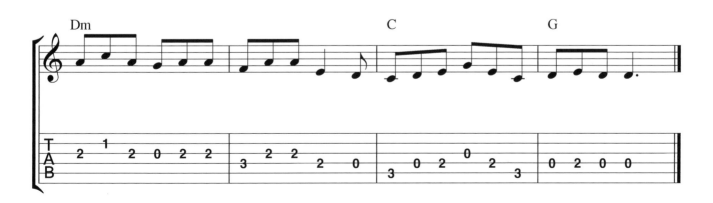

This page has been left blank
to avoid awkward page turns.

Sergeant Early's Jig

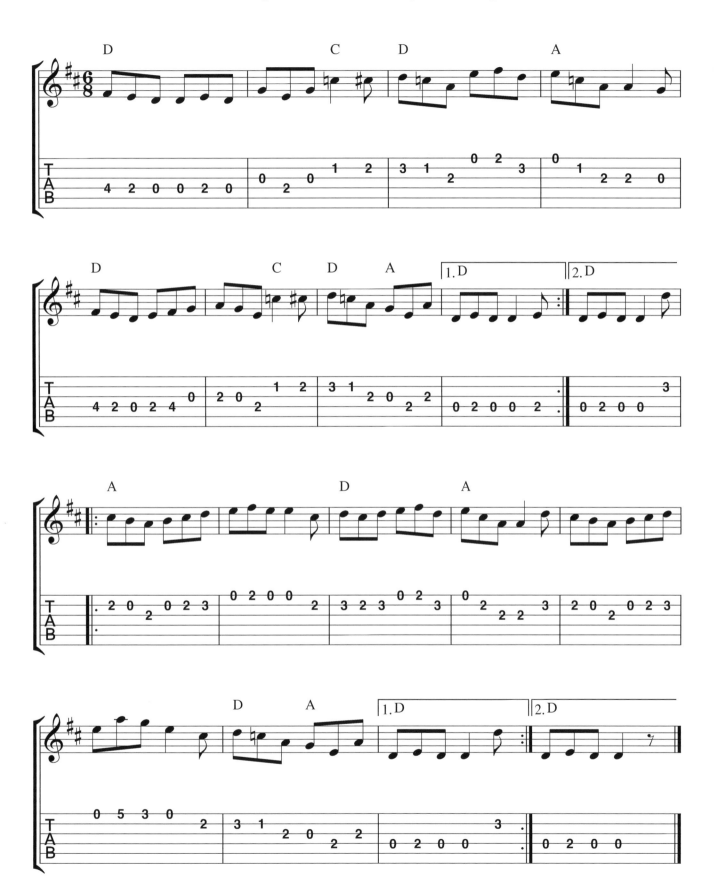

The Jolly Beggarman

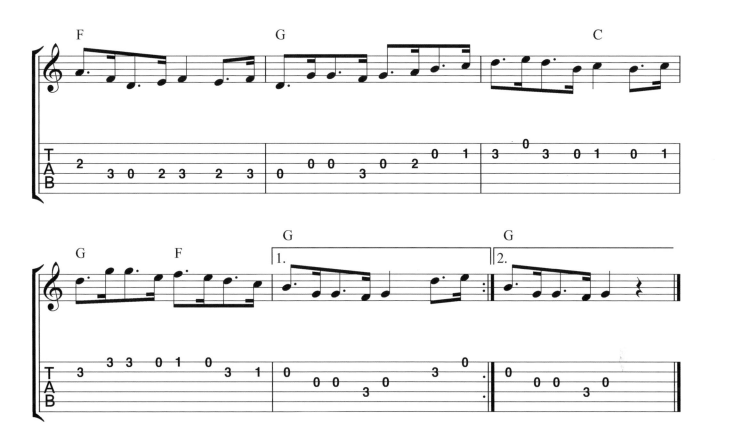

The Rights of Man

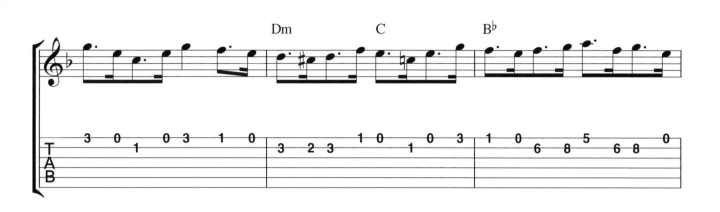

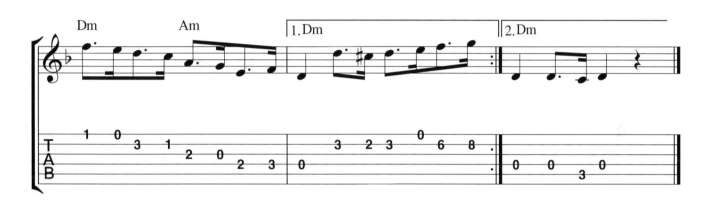

The Wren Hornpipe

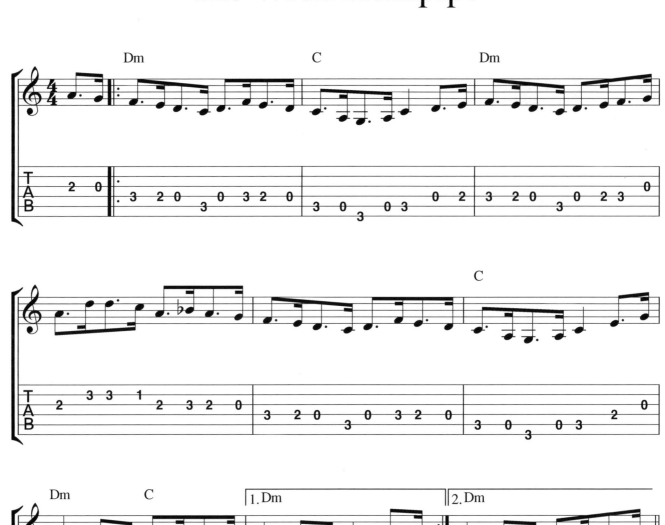

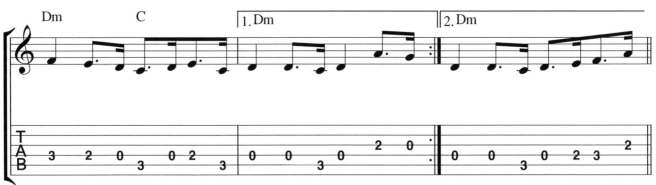

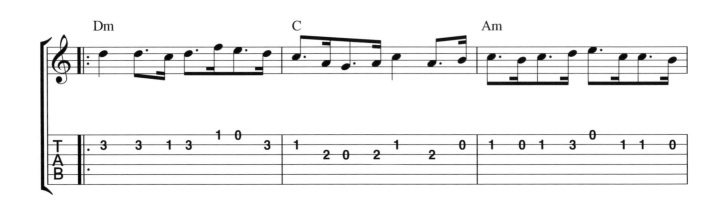

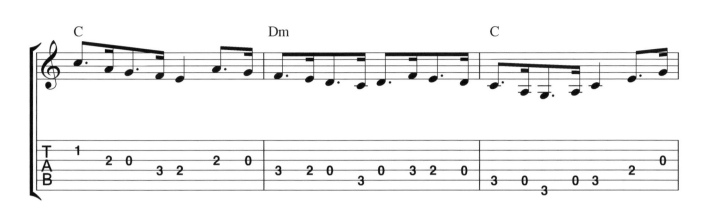

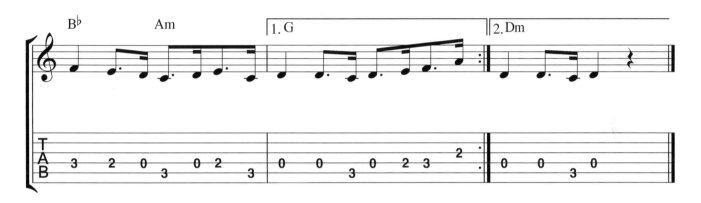

The Boys of Malin

Miss McLeod's Reel

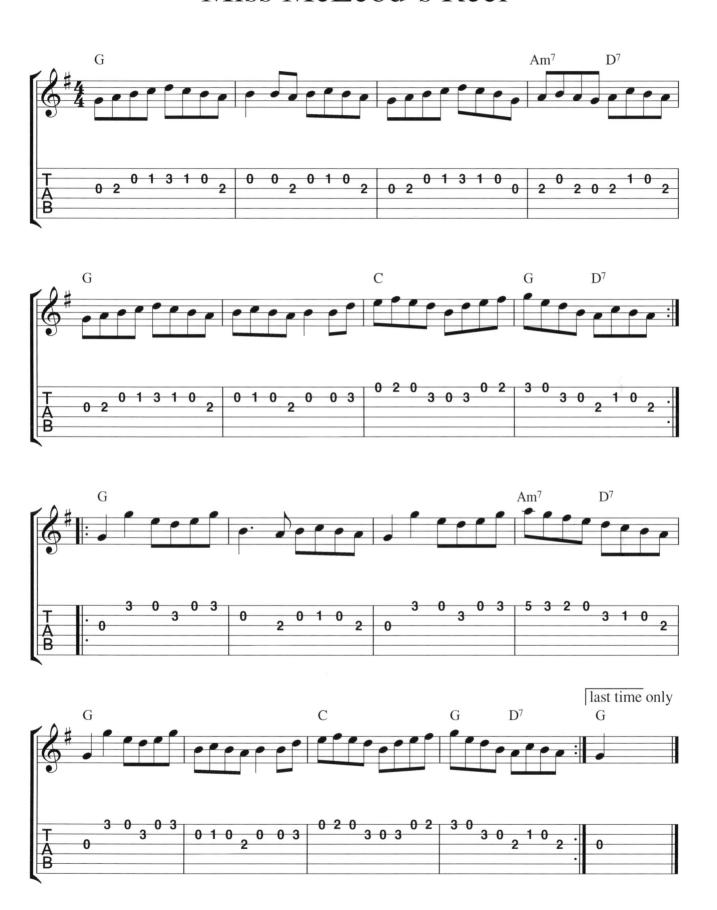

This page has been left blank
to avoid awkward page turns.

The Merry Blacksmith

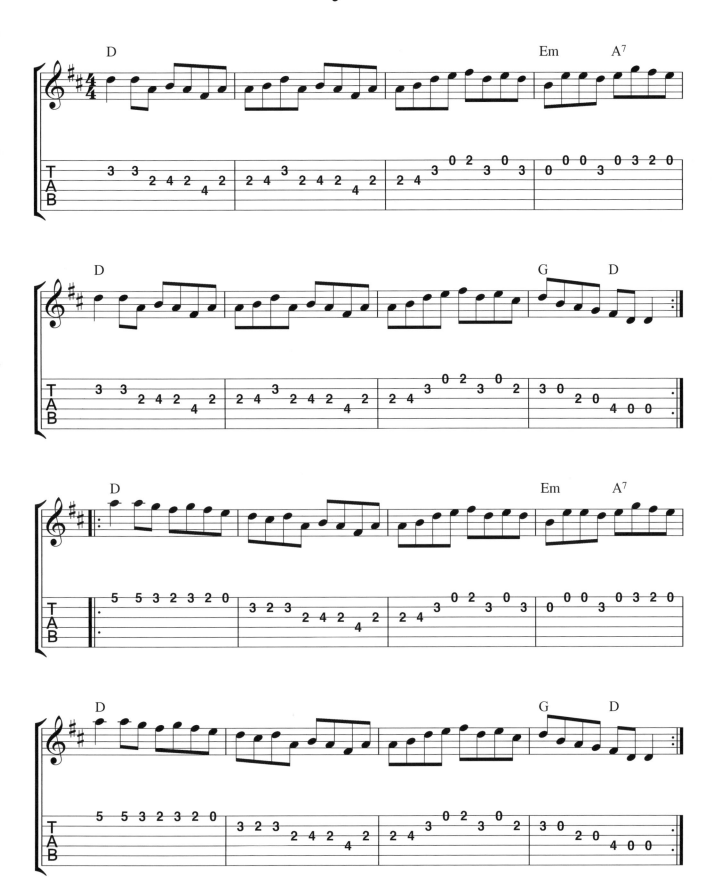

The Star of Munster

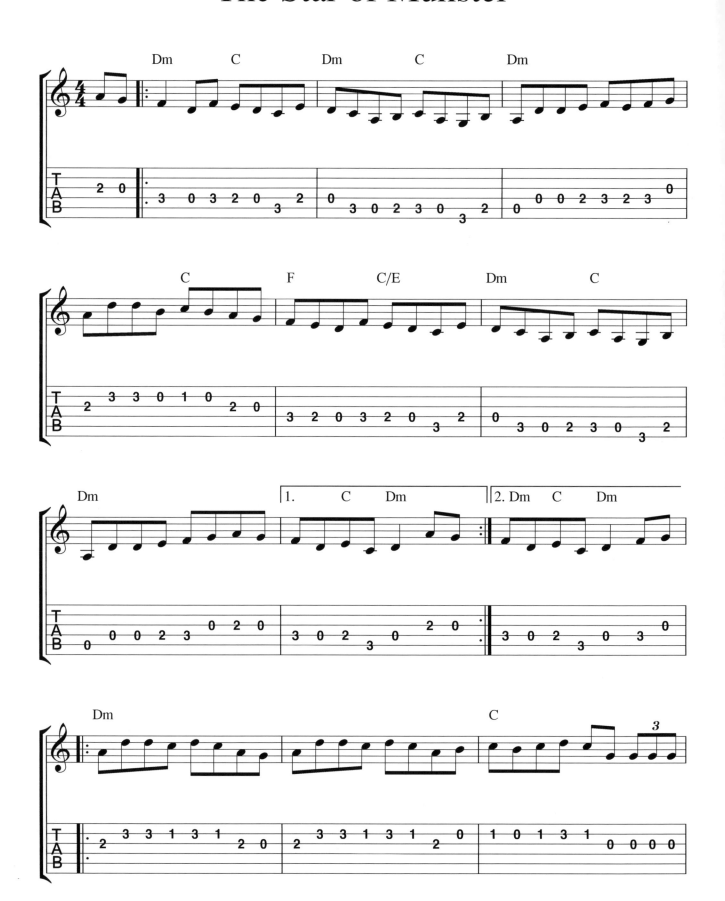

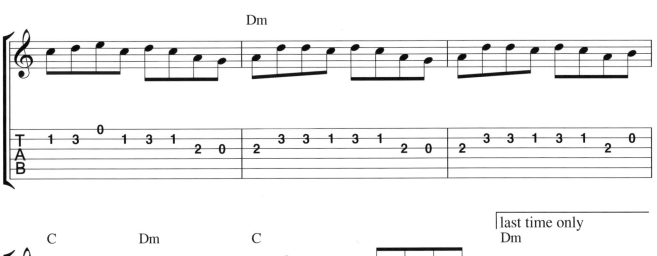

last time only

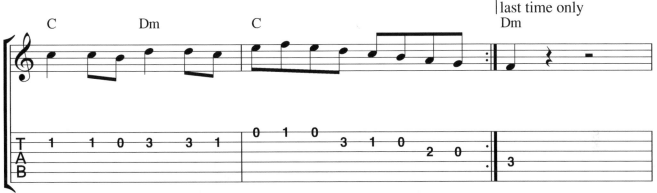

Made in the USA
Coppell, TX
24 January 2021